Teamwork

by Helen Gregory

Consultant:
Adria F. Klein, PhD
California State University, San Bernardino

CAPSTONE PRESS
a capstone imprint

Wonder Readers are published by Capstone Press,
1710 Roe Crest Drive, North Mankato, Minnesota 56003.
www.capstonepub.com

Library of Congress Cataloging-in-Publication Data
Gregory, Helen.
  Teamwork / Helen Gregory.
    p. cm.—(Wonder readers)
  Includes index.
  ISBN 978-1-4765-0041-6 (library binding)
  ISBN 978-1-4296-7898-8 (paperback)
  ISBN 978-1-4765-0856-6 (eBook PDF)
  1. Teams in the workplace—Juvenile literature. 2. Social groups—Juvenile literature. I. Title.
  HD66.G737 2013
  302.3—dc23   2011023873

Summary: Describes how teamwork can help make jobs faster and easier.

Editorial Credits
Maryellen Gregoire, project director; Mary Lindeen, consulting editor; Gene Bentdahl, designer;
Sarah Schuette, editor; Wanda Winch, media researcher; Eric Manske, production specialist

Photo Credits
All Photos Capstone Studio: Karon Dubke except, Shutterstock/Blue Ice, 6; Four Oaks, 14; Hedrus, 15; Kirk
Geisler, 12; Lou Oates, 7; Tan Hung Meng, 13

Word Count: **197**   Guided Reading Level: **G**   Early Intervention Level: **12**

Printed in China.
092012   006934LEOS13

Table of Contents

Note to Parents and Teachers

The Wonder Readers Next Steps: Social Studies series supports national social studies standards. These titles use text structures that support early readers, specifically with a close photo/text match and glossary. Each book is perfectly leveled to support the reader at the right reading level, and the topics are of high interest. Early readers will gain success when they are presented with a book that is of interest to them and is written at the appropriate level.

Working Together

Teamwork means working together.
Teamwork makes our work go faster.

Big jobs go faster with teamwork.
Raking leaves is a big job!

Fighting a fire is a big job. Teamwork makes the job go faster.

Building a house is a big job.
Teamwork makes the job go faster.

Children

Learning to work together takes time.
Children learn to work together
at school.

Children work together to learn.
Teamwork makes learning
science easier.

Children work together when they save the earth. Teamwork makes **recycling** easier.

Children work together when they do **chores**. Teamwork makes playing sports more fun.

Animals

Dogs on a sled team work together. Teamwork makes pulling a heavy load easier.

These ants are working together.
It takes teamwork to get up to
high places.

Elephants need help from each other to stay cool. Teamwork makes it easier to stay cool.

The wildebeest and zebra work together. The zebra can see danger better. The wildebeest is safer near the zebra.

Families

Everyone helps out when families
work together. This family is carving
a pumpkin. Teamwork makes the
job go faster.

This boy and his dad work together on **homework**. Teamwork makes doing homework easier.

Teamwork can also be fun!

Now Try This!

Try working together as a team to play a game, practice math skills, build something, or even clean up the classroom or playground. Before you begin, talk about what makes good teamwork. After you've finished, talk with your team about how well you worked together.

Glossary

chore
a job that has to be done regularly; washing dishes and taking out the garbage are chores

homework
school assignments that your teacher asks you to do at home

recycling
the process of using things again instead of throwing them away

science
the study of the physical world by testing, doing experiments, and measuring

Internet Sites

FactHound offers a safe, fun way to find Internet sites related to this book. All of the sites on FactHound have been researched by our staff.

Here's all you do:

Visit *www.facthound.com*

Type in this code: 9781476500416

Check out projects, games and lots more at
www.capstonekids.com

Index